Progress with Oxford

Age 6-7

Comprehension

Hello! I'm Fay.

And I'm Bulle.

Contents

Key

 Circle

 Colour

 Draw

 Find the sticker

 Match

 Play together

 Read

 Write

OXFORD
UNIVERSITY PRESS

Little Lee

 Little Lee was very, *very* little. She was so little that she had to stand on tiptoe to reach the button when she wanted to cross the road.

 Which of these is Little Lee? Circle the correct picture.

 Little Lee had short brown hair that stuck up in spikes. She had a little nose and little green eyes. She wore little boots and little shorts and a little green T-shirt – or a little blue T-shirt if the little green one was dirty.

 Draw a picture of Little Lee.

 Colour your picture.

But there was something very surprising about Little Lee...

Look carefully at the picture to find the answers.

 Tick the correct answers. Tick one box for each question.

What was surprising about Little Lee?

her little nose ☐

her big voice ☐

her terrible dancing ☐

Why was that surprising?

because she is little ☐

because she hasn't told anyone ☐

because she sings badly ☐

What sort of people liked Little Lee's songs?

old people ☐

young people ☐

old and young people ☐

Well done!

Give yourself a sticker

3

Now – track how you're doing on page 32!

Longer playtimes

3 Hill End
Pixham

12th October

Dear Mrs Arms

I am writing to ask if playtime could be longer. We like playing and my mum says it is healthy to run outside lots.

From
Anna

What do you think Mrs Arms will do?

 Circle the correct answers.

Who wrote this letter?

Mrs Arms   Octavia   Anna

In which month did Anna write her letter?

October   November   December

What does Anna want to be longer?

Maths lessons   Playtime   Art lessons

You could ask for longer playtimes or more pocket money!

 Play with writing.

Write a letter to someone to ask for a change.

Match the words and phrases that mean the same thing.

sadly	good for you
quite right	unhappily
healthy	correct

 Find the words on the blue background in the letter below. Underline them. One is done for you.

Hill Rise Primary School
Pixham

14th October

Dear Anna

Thank you for your letter. You are quite right that it is healthy to play outside and I hope you play outside as much as you can at home.

Sadly, there is not enough time at school to give you more time to play.

Yours sincerely,
B. Arms
Mrs Arms

'Yours sincerely' is a more formal way to finish a letter.

Give yourself a sticker

 Write your answer.

How many days did Mrs Arms take to write to Anna?	
Does Mrs Arms say that she will make playtime longer?	

Now – track how you're doing on page 32!

Mud

How old do you think the poet is? Why?

Mud is very nice to feel
All squishy-squash between the toes!
I'd rather wade in wiggly mud
Than smell a yellow rose.

Nobody else but the rosebush knows
How nice mud feels
Between the toes.

by Polly Chase Boyden

 Circle the correct answer.

Where does the poet say it is nice to feel mud?

under the feet   between the toes   in the fingers

 Why is 'wiggly' a good word to describe the mud?
Tick three reasons.

It starts with the same letter as 'wade'. ☐

It rhymes with 'yellow'. ☐

It describes how the mud feels. ☐

It describes how the mud smells. ☐

It's a more interesting word than 'dirty'. ☐

Would you like to wiggle your toes in mud?

Find the sticker which shows your answer.

Wear your sticker!

Three wise men of Gotham

Three wise men of Gotham
Went to sea in a bowl:
And if the bowl had been stronger
My song would have been longer.

Anon

'Anon' is short for 'anonymous'. It means no one knows who wrote the poem.

 Tick the correct answers. Tick one box for each question.

Where did the wise men come from?

the sea ☐

Gotham ☐

the poem doesn't say ☐

What did the wise men go to sea in?

☐　☐　☐

What do you think happened to the three wise men?

They sank into the sea. ☐

They sailed to a faraway land. ☐

They got lost. ☐

Why would the song have been longer if the bowl had been stronger?

Give yourself a sticker

Now – track how you're doing on page 32!

Origami dog face

 Read these instructions, then answer the questions on the next page.

You will need:
A square piece of paper (for example, 10cm × 10cm)
A felt pen
Googly eyes (optional)

Instructions

1. Fold the paper in half.

2. Fold the paper in half again, then open it up so you leave a crease.

3. Fold the corners down so the points sit beside the main shape.

4. Fold up the bottom corner.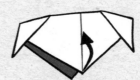

5. Draw on the nose and either stick on the googly eyes or draw on the eyes.

Why are numbers a good idea here?

📖 Read the 'You will need' section of the text.

✏️ Write the answers.

What size is the piece of paper? _____ × _____

Which thing on the list
do you not actually need? _____

📖 Read the 'Instructions' section of the text.

✏️ Write the correct instruction numbers.

This instruction makes the dog's ears. **3**

This instruction turns the square into a triangle. ☐

This instruction makes the dog's nose. ☐

✏️ Can you fill in the missing word in this sentence?

Origami is the art of folding _____
to make shapes or decorations.

 Play with reading.

Follow the instructions to make
an origami dog!

There are stickers
on the sticker sheet
for the dog's eyes.

Give
yourself
a sticker

Now – track how you're doing on page 32!

Tit for tat

There was once a beggar who knocked on the door of a rich man's home hoping to be given something to eat. The rich man ordered his cook to make a bowl of soup for the beggar.

The beggar took the bowl of soup in both hands and had very soon drunk the lot.

Seeing that the man must have been very hungry, the rich man asked, 'Would you like some more?'

'Thank you,' said the beggar, 'but I have had enough.'

 Write the words to complete the sentences.

Use the words from the box.

soup	eat	beggar

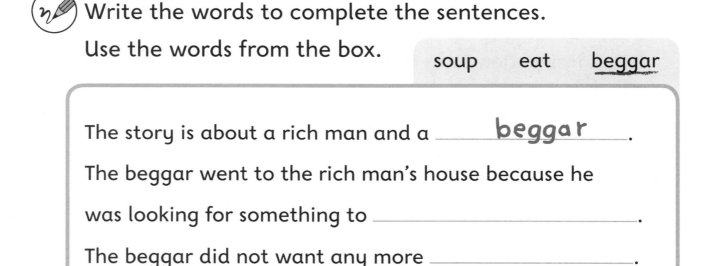

The story is about a rich man and a _____**beggar**_____.

The beggar went to the rich man's house because he

was looking for something to _____.

The beggar did not want any more _____.

Tick the correct answer.

Why did the rich man think the beggar must be very hungry?

Because the beggar didn't want any more soup. ☐

Because the beggar drank all the soup so quickly. ☐

Because the beggar said he was starving. ☐

Next, the rich man placed a plate of chicken in front of the beggar. The beggar ate it so quickly that the rich man asked, 'Would you like some more?'

'Thank you,' said the beggar, 'but I have had enough.'

Then the rich man put a tray of cakes on the table and the beggar ate every one of them.

The rich man was angry and he pushed the beggar. 'Why do you lie to me? Every time I ask you if you want more, you tell me that you have had enough. Then you continue to eat everything I give you.'

Write the words to complete the sentences.

Use the words from the box.

lied	cross	pushed

The rich man _____ the

beggar because he felt _____.

He thought the beggar had

_____ to him.

Do you think the beggar has lied?

The story continues on the next page.

Tit for tat (continued)

The beggar walked to the corner of the room and picked up a box. He tipped stones in until they reached the top of the box. 'Sir,' he said to the rich man, 'is this box full?'

'Of course it is,' said the rich man.

Then the beggar poured sand into the box, which flowed around the stones. He asked again, 'Sir, is this box full?'

'You can see for yourself it is,' said the rich man.

Finally, the beggar poured water over the sand and stones so that the box was now full of stones and sand and water.

What three things did the beggar put into the box? Write your answers.

1. _____

2. _____

3. _____

What do you think will happen next?

_____

_____

_____

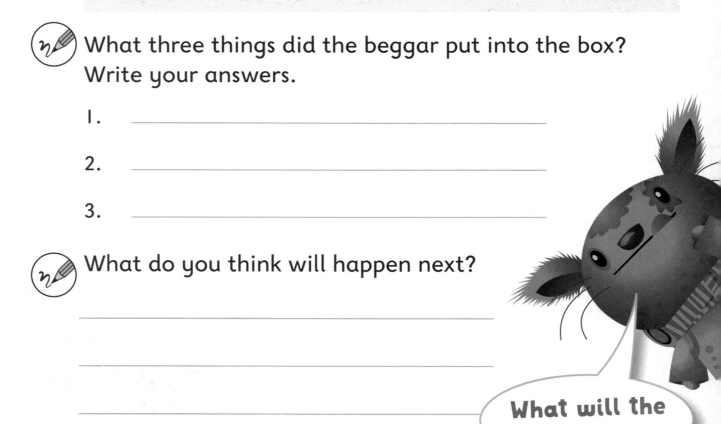

What will the rich man do?

Play with reading.

This is a traditional story from a country called Latvia. Look for Latvia on a map. What else can you find out about Latvia?

The beggar reached over and pushed the rich man. 'Tit for tat!' he said. 'Just as you could not tell if the box was full, I was not able to tell if I had had enough to eat.'

The rich man was very quiet for a moment. Then he laughed and invited the beggar to drink a coffee with him in front of the warm fire.

 Tick the correct answers. Tick one box for each question.

'Tit for tat' means...

eating as much as you can. ☐

giving someone the same punishment that you received. ☐

giving money or food to poor people. ☐

At the end, the rich man feels...

friendly towards the beggar. ☐

angry at the beggar. ☐

ready for his own dinner. ☐

 Underline the sentences in the story that explain your answers.

Ask an adult to help you.

Give yourself a sticker

 Play with reading.

See if you can do the beggar's trick by filling a box or a jar with stones, then sand, then water.

Now – track how you're doing on page 32!

A baby panda

Congratulations, Mulan!

Last Wednesday, the 12th of June, Mulan the giant panda gave birth to a baby daughter!

Giant pandas live in the wild in China but they are an endangered animal. Ten-year-old Mulan lives on a **panda reserve** where twenty-four

Panda cubs playing at the reserve.

of the peaceful bears are looked after. The reserve has nineteen adults, four cubs – and now one baby!

Mulan, who was also born on the reserve, weighs 96kg, but her tiny baby weighs just 100g and is only 12cm long. This is Mulan's second baby. Her first was a male called Yun Long.

The reserve is asking the public to suggest names for the new baby.

A **panda reserve** is a safe place for pandas to live where people protect and look after the pandas.

 Write the answers.

When was the baby panda born? _____

Is the new baby a boy or a girl? _____

How do you know? _____

Are pandas fierce or gentle? _____

Which word tells you that? _____

What is the name of the
baby panda's big brother? _____

✎ Tick all the features that are used in the text.

heading ☐   caption ☐   glossary ☐   labels ☐

✎ Tick the correct answer.

An 'endangered animal' is...

at risk of dying out. ☐

dangerous to people. ☐

Look for clues in the text.

◐ Find the stickers to put in the correct boxes.

Baby panda   **Panda cub**   **Adult panda**

Play with weights.

A baby panda is very light, about 100g.
Find a package in the kitchen that weighs
100g or weigh out 100g of pasta or sugar.

Use a ruler to help you find something
that is 12cm long, the same length as a
baby panda.

Give yourself a sticker

Now – track how you're doing on page 32!

The day out

On Saturday, we went to the nature reserve. It was better than it sounds...

When we arrived, the grown-ups drank coffee while the children explored. First, we climbed trees, then we messed around on the zipwire.

After about an hour, the grown-ups called us back and made us all go on a really long and really boring walk. By the time we got back, I was STARVING.

We had a picnic (crisps and cakes!) then the grown-ups drank more coffee while the kids spent the whole afternoon making The Most Awesome Den EVER in the woods.

On the way home, we stopped to get fish and chips. I was too tired to even eat.

Before bed, Dad made me have a shower. Actually, even I think I needed one. It was a surprisingly good day.

Did the writer expect the trip to the nature reserve to be as much fun as it was?

Look at the second and the last sentences.

Stickers for page 6

I would like to wiggle my toes in mud!

I would NOT like to wiggle my toes in mud!

Stickers for page 9

Stickers for page 15

Stickers for page 25

Character stickers

Reward stickers

Character stickers

Number the pictures to show the order of the events in the story.

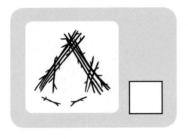

1

 Write three phrases from the text that describe **when** something happened.

1. _____

2. _____

3. _____

 Write your answers.

What was the writer's favourite part of the day?

_____

_____

Why do you think that?_____

_____

Give yourself a sticker

Now – track how you're doing on page 32!

Pete and Mikey

'Pete, play with Mikey in the garden for a moment while I make a phone call,' Mum said.

Pete was ten. His little brother, Mikey, was six – and very annoying.

'Do I have to?' Pete asked.

'Yes!' said Mum. 'I won't be long.'

Circle the correct words to complete the sentences.

Mikey is (six) / ten.

Pete does / does not want to play with Mikey.

Pete is / is not enjoying the video game. I can tell because he is smiling / crying.

Most of the answers are in the pictures.

 Write the words to complete the sentences. Use the words and phrases from the box.

| doesn't notice | Mum | busy | angry | doesn't help |

Pete is not doing what _____ asked him

to do. If she knew, she would be _____.

Pete _____ Mikey because he doesn't

know Mikey is in trouble. He is too _____

playing his video game and _____.

 Write what you think will happen next.

_____

_____

 Now turn the page to find out.

The story continues on the next page.

Sometimes there is no right or wrong answer. But you need to give a reason for your answer.

Pete and Mikey (continued)

'Thanks, Pete,' Mum said when she came back out. 'It's fun playing outside, isn't it? Better than video games! Shall I bring you both something to eat and drink?'

 Write your answers.

Write one word to describe how you think Pete feels when he sees Mikey in trouble.

Who lets Pete know that Mikey is in trouble?

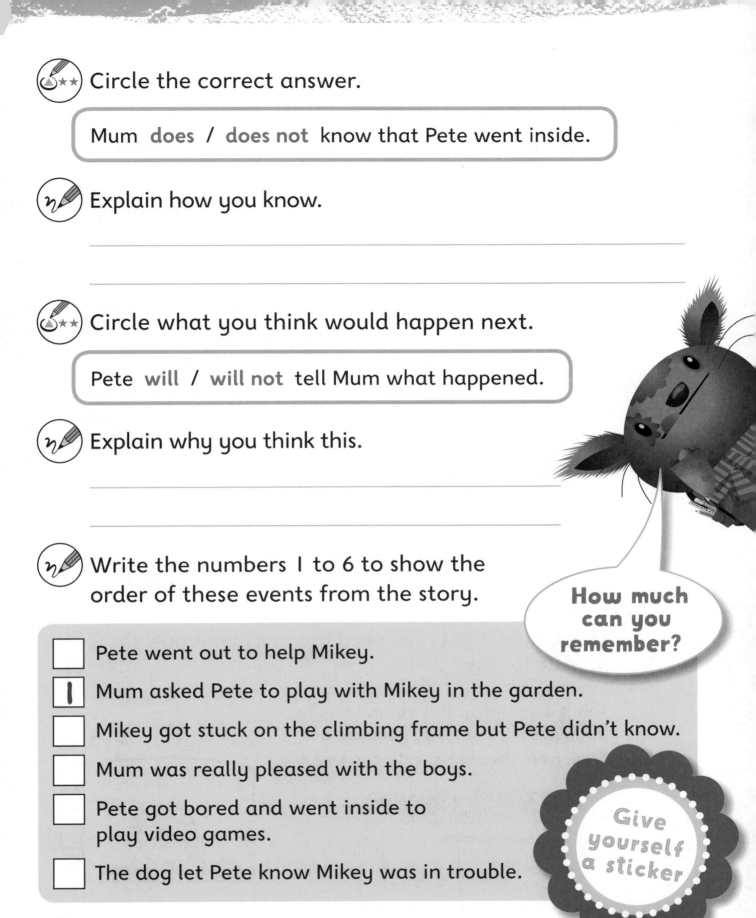

Circle the correct answer.

> Mum **does** / **does not** know that Pete went inside.

Explain how you know.

_____

_____

Circle what you think would happen next.

> Pete **will** / **will not** tell Mum what happened.

Explain why you think this.

_____

_____

Write the numbers 1 to 6 to show the order of these events from the story.

How much can you remember?

☐ Pete went out to help Mikey.

1 Mum asked Pete to play with Mikey in the garden.

☐ Mikey got stuck on the climbing frame but Pete didn't know.

☐ Mum was really pleased with the boys.

☐ Pete got bored and went inside to play video games.

☐ The dog let Pete know Mikey was in trouble.

Give yourself a sticker

Play with storytelling.

Write or tell the story in your own words. Include details about what people said and how they felt.

Now – track how you're doing on page 32!

The basic needs of animals

All animals, including humans, have the same basic needs to survive.

- **Oxygen** Humans and other mammals breathe in air.

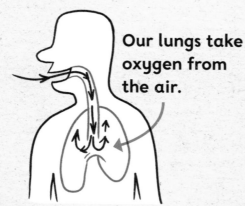

Our lungs take oxygen from the air.

Fish have gills to get oxygen from the water.

- **Water** Most animals drink water. Fish absorb water through their skin.
- **Food** Some animals eat plants while others eat meat. Some animals, like humans, eat both plants and meat.
- **Shelter** Animals need to shelter from the cold or from the heat.

If you have a pet, you need to think about how to provide for their needs.

This is a wormery. The worms breathe through their skin. They get food and drink from the plants rotting in the soil.

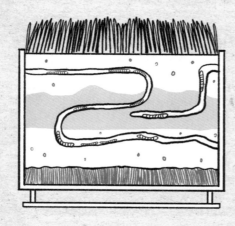

This hamster feels safe in its shelter and sleeps there.

What four things do animals need to survive?

Which do you think is the most important?

1. _____

2. _____

3. _____

4. _____

Write three different ways that animals get oxygen.

1. Humans and mammals

_____

2. Fish

_____

3. Worms

_____

Tick all the features that are used in the text.

bullet points ☐   labels ☐
captions ☐   glossary ☐

Describe how you would provide for the needs of a pet cat.

_____

_____

_____

_____

Give yourself a sticker

Now – track how you're doing on page 32!

Staying healthy

To stay healthy you must:

1. Eat a variety of different foods:

Proteins for muscles and growth

Carbohydrates for energy

Dairy for teeth and bones

Cakes and sweets also provide energy – but you shouldn't have too many of those!

Vitamins to keep your body working properly

2. Drink plenty of water: Water is the best thing to drink.

3. Exercise: Exercise is important to keep your body strong – not just your muscles but also your heart and lungs.

In fact, your heart *is* a muscle!

4. Stay clean: Washing your hands before meals helps avoid tummy bugs.

5. Sleep: A seven-year-old needs about ten-and-a-half hours of sleep every night.

Match the food stickers to the correct food group.

( ) ( ) ( ) ( )

protein   dairy   carbohydrates   vitamins

 Write the words to complete the sentences.

Use words from the box.

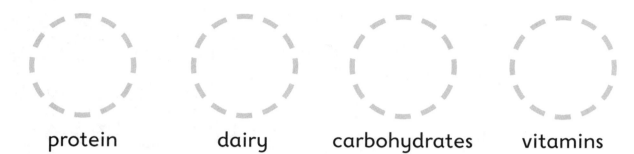 **Think about what you already know, as well as the information in the text.**

germs   sugar   hair   dirt   proteins

_____ are important for growth.

We shouldn't eat too many sweets or cakes because

they contain a lot of _____.

 Write three different sorts of exercise.

1. _____   2. _____

3. _____

 Explain why washing your hands before you eat helps avoid tummy bugs.

_____

 Play with writing.

Make a poster or leaflet to explain to a giant how to keep a pet human. Use everything you have learned about keeping an animal alive and healthy.

 Give yourself a sticker

Lost

All over the castle walls were jewels that sparkled in the sun, their reflections dancing brightly across the garden. Stretching up from the jewelled walls, the tower pierced the purple clouds like a spear.

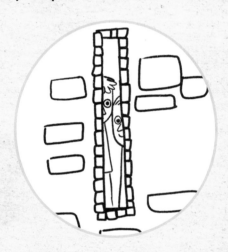

Jay and Swift were not allowed to leave the castle garden but, from their tower window, the brother and sister could look over the garden wall. They could see the faraway golden forest where their baby sister had been lost.

'We'll go there very soon,' Swift said.

'Daddy will never let us,' Jay said.

'He might be king,' Swift said, 'but he can't stop me. I will fly on Zeph to the forest before I am ten!' Zeph was Swift's winged horse.

Jay gasped. 'It's our tenth birthday next week!'

'I leave tomorrow,' Swift said.

Find two details in the story that show the events take place in a fantasy world. Underline them.

Circle the correct answers.

Use a dictionary if you're not sure.

What is on the castle walls?   bricks   snow   jewels

What is the tower like?   fairies   a spear   a tree

What colour is the forest?   golden   purple   silver

What is Swift and Jay's dad?   a soldier   a king   a cook

How old are Swift and Jay?   nine   ten   eleven

 Write your answers.

Find the phrase: *pierced the purple clouds like a spear.*

What do you think 'pierced' means?

_____

What is Zeph?

_____

Swift and Jay are twins. How do you know?

_____

The story continues on the next page.

Why do you think the story is called 'Lost'? What title would you give it?

Lost (continued)

The next morning, Swift rose early, before the sun was up. Jay was waiting for her at the stables.

'I wish I could go with you,' Jay said.

'I know,' Swift said. She led Zeph outside and set free his wings.

Jay limped after his sister. 'Be careful,' he told her.

Swift smiled. 'Of course.'

Lifting his eyes to the sky, Jay watched his sister leave. The two green moons looked on with sad faces.

 Find these words in the text above. Underline them.

one word that means 'got up'

the word that describes how Jay walked

the word that describes the faces of the moons

Use these words to help you answer the next questions.

Answer these questions.

Why do you think Jay cannot go with Swift?

_____

Do you think Swift will come back safely?
Why do you think that?

_____

_____

_____

_____

 Draw Swift riding on Zeph.

There is no right answer – just write what you think.

Give yourself a sticker

 Play with writing.

What do you think happens next? Write an ending for the story and draw a picture to illustrate it.

29

Now – track how you're doing on page 32!

Be a meaning detective

 Read the sentences.

 Circle the correct answers.

Underline the clues in the text that helped you work out your answers.

Otto put his head on Anna's lap and purred.

Otto is: a horse   a dog   a cat

Jon turned bright red and told the man he was sorry.

Jon is: sad   happy   embarrassed

Amy gasped. The view below was stunning.

Amy is: on a mountain   at the seaside   at a playground

 Read these sentences then answer the questions.

Petra's woolly hat made her head itch but she was pleased her dad had put it on her. She threw open the door and ran out to play in the dazzling white world.

 What is the weather like? Circle your answer.

cold and snowy   hot and sunny   wet and windy

 How old do you think Petra is? Circle your answer.

1 year old   67 years old   6 years old

My reading diary

Use the table to write notes about books you have read or had read to you.

Colour the stars to rate each book.

Book title and author Is there an illustrator?	Star rating	Comments
	☆☆☆☆☆	
	☆☆☆☆☆	
	☆☆☆☆☆	

For comments, you could put the name of a favourite character, a word or sentence you liked, a fact that interested you or anything the book made you think of.

Give yourself a sticker

Now – track how you're doing on page 32!

Progress Chart

 Colour me in!

😊	I can do this well
😐	I can do this but need more practice
🙁	I find this difficult

Page	I can . . .	How did you do?
2–3	I can read and answer questions about a character description.	😊 😐 🙁
4–5	I can read and understand letters, and discuss and explain ideas.	😊 😐 🙁
6–7	I can read and understand poetry, and think about interesting word choices.	😊 😐 🙁
8–9	I can read and understand an instruction text, and think about why some text features are helpful.	😊 😐 🙁
10–13	I can read and understand a traditional tale, and predict what might happen next.	😊 😐 🙁
14–15	I can read and understand a report text, and interpret the text.	😊 😐 🙁
16–17	I can read and understand a recount text, and put the events in sequence.	😊 😐 🙁
18–21	I can read and understand a story with a familiar setting, and discuss and explain ideas.	😊 😐 🙁
22–23	I can read and understand an information text, and talk about the structure of non-fiction texts.	😊 😐 🙁
24–25	I can read and understand an information text, and use things I already know to help me answer questions.	😊 😐 🙁
26–29	I can read and understand a fantasy story and think about word choices.	😊 😐 🙁
30–31	I can use details to understand the meaning of a text, and talk about the sorts of books I like to read.	😊 😐 🙁

How did YOU do?